My Secret Life Being A Pastor's Wife

Sandra E. Weekes

ISBN: 978-1-938950-66-7
Editor: Shari Armstrong
Interior Design: Tony Bradford

Greater is He Publishing
9824 E. Washington St,
Chagrin Falls Ohio 44023
P O. Box 46115
Bedford Ohio, 44146

Dedication

I write this testimony in dedication to my fellow sisters in Christ, the Elect Women of God all over this nation. You were elected, anointed, and appointed by God to stand. Yes, my sisters, sometimes to stand alone. *"Wherefore take unto you the whole armour of God that ye may be able to withstand in the evil day, and having done all, to stand.*
14 Stand therefore, having your loins girt about with truth, and having on the breastplate of righteousness." *(Ephesians 6:13-14 KJV)*
 I have prayed, my sisters, as you read my testimony, that you will feel the love and compassion of my heart for each and every one of you who has lived a similar life. Please allow me to encourage you to live. *"Trust in the Lord with all thine heart; and lean not unto thine own understanding. 6 In all thy ways acknowledge him and he shall direct thy paths."* *(Proverbs 3:5-6 KJV)*
 When I allow these Scriptures to saturate my spirit, God begins to move, deliver, heal, and set free. We know according to the word: *"Then Peter opened his mouth, and said, Of a truth I perceive that God is no respecter of persons: (Acts 10:34 KJV).*

For information about the author see her website:
www.wavevi.org.

CONTENTS

CHAPTER 1
The Beginning -
Relationship in the Making

In an attempt to share my story, I asked the Lord, "Where do I start? It's so much to share." The Lord said to me, "How about the beginning?" So as I reflected back on my married life, it had its ups and downs as most marriages do. When it was good, it was very good. However, when it was bad, it was terrible. My life was the opposite of what I thought life would be being a pastor's wife. I knew what I imagined and what I pictured. But to my surprise, my first fourteen months were not even close. What was so amazing to me was that people were actually jealous of what I call the "display."

Display: to engage in a stereotyped behavior that conveys information to individuals of the same or another species.

Species: a class of individuals having some common characteristics or qualities; distinct sort or kind.

It all started in mid-September of 2013. We had a guest pastor at church on Wednesday night. Although he was not the speaker, Bishop allowed him to say a few words to the church. As I sat at the credit card machine assisting with the offering, I could see this guest pastor on the big screen. He began to tell the church that when you pray, you must be specific with the Lord. He went on to say that he had told the Lord what he wanted specifically in a wife. He told the Lord how tall, how dark, how long he wanted her hair to be, and he even told the Lord what size he wanted her to be. While many people said "amen" and others chuckled, I sat in the back and said, "Lord, he has told you he wanted me." I knew in my spirit he was describing me to the Lord. After listening to him, I laughed to myself and said he swears he is talking about me, but the devil is a liar.

As Bishop was exiting the church, he saw me sitting in the corner and said, "I need to see you in my office." I followed him into his office, and as I sat down I became a little nervous. Bishop sat on the sofa across from me and said, "I need to ask you a question."

Okay.

To my surprise, Bishop asked, "What do you think about Apostle Weekes?"

I quickly responded, "Absolutely nothing!"

Bishop laughed. "Really?"

I had no idea where this conversation was going, but I could tell Bishop was somewhat confused by my answer because he had been told by Apostle Weekes what he thought about me, but the feelings were not mutual.

I told Bishop, "I've known him a very long time; we are friends and he's a nice guy. Other than that, I don't think anything else."

Bishop said, "Okay," and I left his office.

I left out confused and asking myself, "Where did that come from?" As I entered back into the sanctuary, Apostle Weekes was coming down the aisle headed to Bishop's office. We stopped in the aisle to greet one another, and I was thinking about the short conversation I'd just had with Bishop.

After a two minute conversation in the middle of the aisle, Apostle Weekes said, "May I have your phone number?"

I replied, "No, Sir."

He laughed and said, "I am returning to the Virgin Islands and would really like your number."

I told him, "That's not a good idea."

However, he did not give up. "Okay. How about I give you my number?"

I said, "That's fine, although I probably won't use it."

He said, "That's okay, just take it."

So I did. However, when I reached home I threw it away. I wasn't the least bit interested. I had set myself aside to live and wait on the Lord for my husband. I wasn't taking any chances on dating and missing who God had for me, not knowing he was God's choice.

After being called into Bishop's office again, my answer was still the same concerning this matter. Finally, Bishop said to me, "Woman of God, I know that you hear from God. I'm going to suggest to you that you enter into prayer concerning Apostle Weekes."

I said, "Wow, Bishop, do I have to?"

Bishop sat up on the sofa and said to me in a very clear voice, "If you don't, you're going to miss what God has for you." He went on to tell me that every time he sees Apostle Weekes, he sees me standing next to him in the spirit.

All I could say was, "Jesus!" A couple of weeks before this conversation with Bishop, the Lord had said to me in six a.m. prayer, "Don't miss my Glory." I sat back on the loveseat in disbelief. I knew Bishop was on point to what God had already spoken to me. Bishop began to minister to me on how people make mistakes and how people change. He spoke on God's grace and the things God will do for the sake of ministry. By the time Bishop finished with this fifteen-minute conversation, I knew I had to pray immediately. I knew whatever God was doing, I didn't want to miss it.

I obeyed the voice and instructions of my pastor. We had prayer at the church Monday through Friday at six a.m. However, I felt that I needed to enter the sanctuary before everyone else to lie on my face before God. That is exactly what I did. I called my prayer partner, Mother Jessie Gaither, and asked her, "Could you please take me to the church at five o'clock to pray instead of six?" I explained to her that Bishop had given me something to pray on and I needed to get there before the group. With her sweet little voice, she said, "Of course I can. It must be really important if you want to get there that early."

I told her, "It's so important I can't even talk about it right now. I just know I need to get into God's presence without any distractions."

The next morning, Mother Jessie arrived at my daughter's apartment, where I was staying, promptly at four forty-five. We arrived at the church at five o'clock. As Mother Jessie began to unlock the doors of the church, I felt nervous. I slowly entered the church and briefly stood in the vestibule. I said, "Have your way, Lord," and entered the sanctuary. I began walking around the church and worshiping God. Then I said, "God, everything I once knew, and everything I think I know of Apostle Weekes, please clear my mind. Erase the past. Take it away from me, God. I've known him almost twenty years, so, God, I need your help."

I told the Lord to show me the man he was and the man He was calling him to be. Lo and behold, God did exactly what I petitioned him to do. He showed me his imperfection, issues, struggles, and his strengths. He showed me his desire to live for God with a wife that could compliment his weakness. God showed me the man of God He was calling him to be. The man He was going to use to deliver many souls. The man He was sending to the nations to preach and teach the glorious gospel of Jesus Christ.

I began to cry before the Lord. No, not because I was happy. I was sad, disappointed, and mad at the things God had shown me. I did not comprehend how, after all these years, God was telling me this man was to be my husband. I said, "Lord, he can't be."

The Lord said, "Yes, Daughter."

I said, "No, God! No! No! No!" Although I was preparing myself physically and spiritually for my husband, I was having a difficult time accepting what I was preparing myself for over the past year and a half.

However, I have always been a girl of many questions when it comes to the things of the Lord concerning my life. So I had to have a question and answer session with God. I needed some understanding.

Proverbs 4:7 *Wisdom is the principal thing; therefore, get wisdom: and with all thy getting get understanding.*

I sat before the Lord and began to ask him these questions:

Why Lord?

Why me?

Why him?

Why now?

What the Lord spoke in response blew me away. He said to me, "This man of God has purposed it in his heart to live and walk upright before Me. Because of this, according to My Word, I must give him his heart's desire."

"Delight thyself also in the Lord; and he shall give thee the desires of thine heart" (Psalm 37:4).

I said, "Oh, my God." I am his heart's desire.

The Lord said, "Yes, Daughter, calm yourself and let Me

share some things with you." That moment, the Lord began to show me the better picture of what my marriage would be. The Lord spoke these words to my spirit: "I have made you the desire of his heart because I chose you to walk alongside this man of God. However, you will walk as one in the Spirit. So you will know and understand that it is I who has done this, you will have the same exact initials to represent your oneness in Me, S.E.W. When people see him, they will see you. When they hear him, they will hear you, and vice versa." He went on to say, "Look at his initials, S.E.W. What does that spell? What does that mean?" He said, "Sew means to join together, to attach, to mend. I will sew you together as fabric, and what I have sewed, joined, no man or woman will be able to separate."

I began to cry again. However, this time, it was tears of joy and thanksgiving. I was thanking God for what He was about to do in my life. I was thanking God for choosing me for this man of God. I gave God praise for revealing my husband to me. Most of all, I gave Him praise for finding favor in me to promote me in His Kingdom as a First lady, as a pastor's wife.

After hearing from God, I was able to share with my bishop the things God had spoken to me in prayer. Bishop was not surprised at all. I was only telling him what God had already shown him. I asked Bishop, "What do I do now?"

To my surprise, Bishop said, "Nothing. You continue to do just what you've been doing, nothing. Don't pursue him; let God do it.

I listened, once again, to Bishop and followed his instructions.

In the meantime, while I waited on God, I continued to seek His face. During this time, God gave me some details, some instructions, some dos and don'ts pertaining to this marriage. He told me I am not to make the same mistakes that some other pastors' wives have made. I am to be submissive to my husband as well as my pastor. He reminded me of Ephesians 5:22, *Wives, submit yourselves unto your own husbands, as unto the Lord.* What He said next, once again, left me asking questions. He said, "Although I called you to submit, don't be stupid. Because you did not submit in your previous marriage, I know you desperately want to get it right this time. However, there is a thin line between submission and stupidity."

I asked, "Lord, how will I know the difference?"

The Lord said to me, "If it lines up with My Word, submit. If it goes against My Word, don't be stupid."

Being naive, I said to the Lord, "But he's an apostle. Surely he won't ask me to do anything that goes against Your Word?" Or so I thought.

The Lord said, "Don't be blinded by the title; he's still a man."

At that point, I felt a little discomfort. I began to tell the Lord, "Oh no, You can deliver him from whatever before we get married. God, am I suppose to just settle for that?"

The Lord said to me, "No, Daughter."

I knew you wouldn't settle. From that day, I began to pray for my husband-to-be.

Several weeks later, while driving home from Dothan, AL, I realized I had a missed call and voicemail. When I checked the call log, I did not recognize the number. I thought it was a Virginia number. However, it was a Virgin Islands number. After listening to the voicemail from my would-be husband, I was excited, but at the same time I was wondering, how on earth did he get my phone number? When I returned the call, he informed me he had gotten the number from Bishop, who had to get the number from someone else. He had explained to Bishop that the Lord told him I was his wife and he needed to talk to me before the year ended. So Bishop, knowing what he knew and what I had already shared with him, got my number and passed it on.

So this was the moment we both were waiting for. I heard the phone smile in his voice as he probably could, too. After going through the preliminaries, he told me that he had something to say. He only wanted me to listen until he was finished.

So I said, "Okay."

He proceeded to tell me how he had loved me for years and I never took him seriously. But the Lord spoke to him and told him I was to be his wife. However, this was his last time reaching out to me. He heard God, he trusted God, and he loved me, but if I was not interested, he needed to know so he could move on.

I began to laugh and I told him, "Yes, I know, and I'm not running anymore."

He was going on and on with what the Lord said, and he missed what I said. He paused and said, "Excuse me, what did you say?"

I repeated myself, then there was a moment of silence. I think he dropped the phone. I said, "Hello, hello, are you there?"

Finally, he answered, "Yes dear, I'm here."

"Are you shocked?"

"Yes."

"Why?"

"Because you never responded so quickly before," he said.

Yep, he was right. However, I told him this was the Lord's doing. After many attempts over the years, he finally got the answer he was looking for. Good things come to those who wait. However, wait on the Lord. *"Whoso findeth a wife findeth a good thing and obtaineth favour of the Lord."* (Proverbs 18:22).

"For since the beginning of the world men have not heard, nor perceived by the ear, neither hath the eye seen, O God, beside thee, what he hath prepared for him that waiteth for him." (Isaiah 64:4)

There were many phone conversations, emails, and text messages that took place after that day, every morning, afternoon, night, and sometimes late night. We were getting to know each other. God was building a love in our relationship that only He could do. We talked about everything from the mistakes we made in our previous marriages to ministry, the past, present and our future. The thought of me being a pastor's wife was becoming more exciting.

Then the day came when he invited me to the Virgin Islands to get a feel for what island life would be like for me. I was excited about making the trip. I was even more excited to see his face since we knew I was going to be his wife. However, in all my excitement I sought counsel from my bishop and first lady about taking this trip. After a long conversation of wisdom and guidance, I received the approval I was looking for. Two weeks later, I was on my way to becoming the pastor's wife.

I arrived on the beautiful island of St. Thomas, known to the locals as "The Rock", a day after my forty-fifth birthday. When I exited the plane, I was in awe of God's marvelous work. There was no jetway like most airports. When I exited the plane, it was outside at the gate. The island was so beautiful. I said, "Thank you, God, for my life." I stopped to take pictures; after all, I was a tourist. I continued to walk to reach the other side of the airport. Just as I did, I saw my husband-to-be walking back and forth, looking for me. Like a high school girl in love for the first time, my heart began to flutter. I could not stop smiling. I was trying to calm myself down before he noticed me. I stopped and hid behind a pole. In an effort to calm myself, I called his cell phone. I could hear the excitement in his voice that I was feeling in my heart. I thought, I can't believe this is happening.

He kept saying, "Where are you? Where are you? I don't see you."

I stepped from behind the pole. When he turned and saw me standing there, the biggest smile I've ever seen came over his face. I will never forget that look. He walked over to me, gave me a hug, and reached for my luggage. I didn't know what to expect, but it definitely wasn't that. I began to think he was joking. I know that wasn't it. No big hug, no long kiss, no spin in the air. Oh, he must be playing. I told myself that he didn't want me to know how excited he really was.

I was still excited, but at the same time somewhat disappointed. I had played this over and over again in my head while on the plane. He was going to lift me off my feet, spin me in the air, and kiss me like it was his last chance. I had really imagined a different kind of welcome. He so nicely escorted me to his truck, opened my door, put my luggage in the back seat, and then he got in his seat. We proceeded to leave the airport. Upon exiting the airport gate, he looked at me with a big smile and said, "Welcome to St. Thomas, or should I say, welcome home."

I laughed, still thinking, He can't be serious, just a hug? In my excitement, I was starting to feel a little confused.

Then the Lord said, "Remember, he is a pastor."

"I know, Lord, but I'm his wife."

The Lord said, "You are right, but he's not your husband yet."

I cleared my throat and said, "Yes, Lord."

Then I remembered Bishop saying to me, "You're going to be there four days on this beautiful island; however, don't taint what the Lord is about to do in your life. Continue to wait on God. I know sometimes people get caught up in the atmosphere and what's going on. I've heard everything is an aphrodisiac, but remember, you're not husband and wife yet."

I said, "Thank you, Lord." I had already made up my mind that we were not having sex until we married. However, I thought a kiss would be okay.

The Lord said, "Not so."

"But every man is tempted, when he is drawn away of his own lust, and enticed. Then when lust hath conceived, it brings forth sin: and sin when it is finished, bringeth forth death. Do not err, my beloved brethren." (James 1:14-16)

My first visit to the Virgin Islands was amazing. The island had much to offer. Beautiful beaches, nice shops, great local entertainment, and so much more. The streets were full of tourists who had come on the cruise ships. I saw people walking and drinking out of coconuts. Now, as funny as that looked, I had to have one. After I had it, I haven't desired to have it again. I had a chance to experience the island as a tourist.

Over the next three days, he took me everywhere there was to go. I saw all the major sights, ate at all the best restaurants for breakfast and lunch. He cooked dinner for me every night. We had long walks on the many different beaches. Great conversations about us, our life, our friends, our family, island life, island people, and ministry. I thought, okay, Lord, I could get used to this. I could adapt to change. I can handle the responsibility of being a pastor's wife with the Lord's help. My days seemed to go by so fast.

When the time came for me to return home, I really wanted to stay a few more days. However, I knew it wasn't possible. He said to me "Soon, darling, very soon."

11

All I could do was look at him and smile. I knew in my spirit it would be soon. I knew because this was God's doing and we both trusted the Lord. We would not have a long courtship.

He said to me, "You can leave some of your things here, since you know you're coming back, if you like."

"Okay, I think that's a good idea."

He began to clear out a drawer and made space in the closet for my clothes. I was smiling so hard my face hurt. I just kept thinking, "God, is this real?" As I began to take things out of my packed suitcase, it hit me; this is going to be home for me. I began to cry.

He asked, "Are you okay?"

"Yes," I said through my tears.

"Are you sure?" he asked. "Why are you crying?"

I turned to face him, but before I could answer he said, "I know, Darling, I'm happy also." Then he kissed my forehead and just held me. I was an emotional wreck. I pulled myself together so I could leave for the airport. I don't know why it seemed so hard at the time, but off to the airport we went. Once again, he opened my door, got my luggage out the back, and walked with me to check in. After I checked in, he began to explain to me what it was going to be like going through customs. When he was done, I reached to give him a hug, and the welcome kiss I had anticipated was my goodbye kiss.

"Really, when I'm leaving?"

He chuckled and said, "Yep, you know it."

I said to myself, "God, you know you have a sense of humor." I boarded the plane and returned home, not knowing when or what God was going to do next. But I knew I had to wait on the Lord. I knew I had to have patience. *"But let patience have her perfect work, that ye may be perfect and entire, wanting nothing." (James 1:4)*

The next two months, we talked every day, sometimes four and five times a day. We kept each other informed on our day, what we had going on in our lives at work and at home. We were building a long distance bond that was strengthening our relationship. We both knew at some point, because of ministry, we would be apart. He already traveled much, and I was seeking God's face on being the kind of pastor's wife he called me to be. I desired to be what God wanted me to be and not what the people expected or wanted.

We began to pray every morning on the phone with each other, sharing what God was speaking to us individually. I absolutely loved it because prayer was my thing.

"Pray without ceasing." *(1 Thessalonians 5:17)*

"And he spake a parable unto them to this end, that men ought always to pray, and not to faint." (Luke 18:1)

After much prayer, he told me, "It's time for you to be introduced to the church."

"Why?" I asked.

"The people need to know God has given me my heart's desire," he said.

"It's only right they meet you before and know who their first lady will be. Besides," he said, "the church has been praying for me a wife."

"Oh, really?" I said. Then I asked, "What if they don't approve?"

He said, "Darling, you don't have to worry about that. You are my choice! They don't get to choose for me. I know what I want, and God knows exactly what I need."

"Yes, he does, baby!" I proclaimed. We both had to laugh. "God is giving us both who and what we need."

He agreed.

So we decided I would return to St. Thomas the last week in February and be introduced to the church the first Sunday in March. Once again, I went to seek counsel from my bishop. Once again, he gave me more wisdom and guidance. He clearly told me the Lord was going to do a quick work. "Don't fight it, let God be God and accept what he is doing in your life. "

"Yes, sir."

On February twenty-sixth, I boarded a plane to St. Thomas. This time, however, my level of excitement wasn't the same. I was excited to see him again, although I was somewhat nervous about the church. In the weeks leading up to my return to the islands, I began to seek God concerning the church. I fasted and prayed, believing God for revelation and understanding of where he was sending me. During my time of prayer, the Lord revealed to me that although the church was praying for him a wife, there would be many that wouldn't accept me. The Lord let me know to keep my spiritual eyes and ears open; know the spirits by the spirit. From that warning, I knew this was going to be interesting. But I knew God had my back. God reminded me of who I am in Him. So I was a little nervous, but I was not afraid. *"For I the Lord thy God will hold thy right hand, saying unto thee, Fear not; I will help thee." (Isaiah 41:13)*

I took comfort in knowing God's word shall not return unto Him void. (Isaiah 55:11)

Sunday morning was here. Because he gets to church early, he arranged for his friend to come and pick me up for church. We arrived at the church late. I later learned he had planned it that way. He didn't want anyone to have a chance to find out who I was before he made his announcement. We entered the church, and heads began to turn. The entrance brought us into the middle of the church.

His friend stepped in and reached for my hand, as there was a step inside. I followed his friend to the far side of the church and sat down somewhat near the back. When we got to our seats, his friend leaned over to me and said, "They're trying to figure out who you are and where my wife is."

I laughed and said, "Oh, my. She does know where you are, right?"

Laughing, he said, "Oh, of course."

"Good. I would hate for you to be in trouble trying to help."

"No worries."

I sat and enjoyed the praise and worship although it was quite different from what I was used to. Nevertheless, it was good. Then came time to welcome all first-time visitors. "Uh, oh. What am I going to do now?" I was thinking. He and I hadn't discussed how or when he was going to introduce me. So I decided not to stand.

One of the ushers walked over to me and said, "Is this your first time here?"

I pretended not to hear her.

She tapped me on my shoulder to get my attention and asked again, "Have you been here before?"

I responded, "No I haven't."

"I didn't think so," she said.

I was thinking, "Will you please leave me alone?" But she didn't. She gave me a gift bag and a visitor's card to fill out. I said, "Oh, okay," but then she came back with a mic asking me to stand and tell the church my name and where I was from. I said, "No, thank you," as I was looking to him for some kind of signal as to what to do.

From the pulpit, he nodded as if to say, "Yes, stand up." So I took the mic, because the usher wasn't moving. I began to tell the church, "My name is Ms. Hardaway, and I am a visitor of Patrick's." I didn't tell them where I was from because they know he used to live in Pensacola.

When the usher asked, "Where are you from?" he interrupted so nicely that I didn't have to answer that question. While he was speaking, I sat down and she walked away.

His friend leaned over and told me, "Good job. That was clever."

We both laughed. However, the anticipation of being introduced was still lingering in the air. I wasn't aware he was going to wait until the end of the service. When he finished preaching, they played the announcements. I was getting so antsy. Like can we do this already? Finally, he stood up and said to the congregation he had one more announcement to make. Oh my. My stomach had butterflies instantly.

I leaned to his friend and said, "This is it."

"Are you ready?" he asked.

"Ready or not, it's happening."

He had a small chuckle, looked at me and said, "Yep."

"I told you all last year the Lord was going to give me a wife before my birthday."

The church began shouting, "Yes, yes."

He continued to explain, "The Lord has given me the desire of my heart. The church doesn't have to pray for me a wife anymore. God has answered your prayers."

"The effectual fervent prayer of a righteous man availeth much." (James 5:16)

The church, with joy and excitement, began standing on their feet, clapping their hands, and shouting simultaneously, "Praise the Lord!", "Yes!", and "Amen and thank you, Lord."

When I saw and heard this, my butterflies went away. He told the church his wife-to-be was here today and he wanted to introduce the church to their first lady. He called out, "Sandra, come up here."

I didn't move. I took five seconds to scan their faces.

He looked at me, and while motioning with his hand to

come, he said, "Darling, come to me."

I stood on my feet, held my head up high, and strutted my way down the aisle with a huge smile on my face. However, I could hear that the level of excitement had dropped. I don't know what was going on through the minds of some of the people, but I could imagine. However, it didn't really matter to me at the time. All I knew was that it was the Lord's doing, and it was marvelous in my sight.

As I reached him in the middle of the church, he reached for my hand, pulled me to him, gave me a hug and kiss on the lips, and stated, " I thank God for my good thing." He then called for the ministers to circle around us and pray. As the ministers were coming, I heard the Lord again say, "Keep your Spiritual ears open." From the prayer that went forth, I knew in my spirit even some of them were not as happy as they pretended to be.

"Woe unto you, scribes and Pharisees, hypocrites! for ye devour widows' houses, and for a pretence make long prayer: therefore ye shall receive the greater damnation." (Matthew 23:14)

After the prayer, he closed out service and the people began to flow to the front of the church to greet me. Many came with genuine smiles and hugs and welcomed me to the church family. Some said, "Congratulations." They said that they were really happy for Apostle Weekes While others came with a loose handshake and reserved spirit to say welcome. Since God had already given me a warning, I didn't let that bother me at all.

Then all of a sudden a young lady breaks out singing, "To God be the Glory, To God be the Glory, To God be the Glory for the things He has done."

Then I had a praise break, giving God thanks for His goodness.

The young lady singing gave me a hug that was like no

other. It felt different, it was pure and really from the heart.

I said, "Okay, Lord, who is she?"

After church, we went to eat. On the drive, Apostle Weekes said, "I want you to meet someone, so we are going to eat with some folks."

I first thought, "I really don't want to meet anyone else right now, but okay." So we made it to the restaurant and went inside. To my surprise, it was the young lady from the church who was singing, along with her sister. Now, I'm like, "Okay?" But I remember I did just ask God who she was. So we approached the table. I noticed he was watching my face to see what I was thinking. I kept smiling.

We got to the table, and he looked at me and said, "You remember her from the church?"

"Yes. I was wondering who she was."

He said, "This is my cousin."

I said to myself, "That was the hug that was pure." The Lord let me know that He would reveal the hearts of the people to you if you stay in His presence. He did exactly what he said He would do.

Over the next couple of days, I got a small taste of what being a pastor's wife would be like. I saw him handling phone calls, juggling meetings, going to pray for the sick, and yet he had made time for me while I was there. In the midst of all his pastoral duties, we sat down to discuss a wedding date. While he was pulling up the calendar on his cell phone, I quickly said, "April nineteenth."

He paused and said, "I hope you're not talking about next year."

Laughing, I said, "No, baby. If the nineteenth is on a Saturday, I'm talking about next month." He looked at the calendar, smiled, and said, "Next month it will be. How did you know it was a Saturday?"

"Almost two years ago the Lord told me I would marry on Saturday, April nineteenth. He never said a year."

"Really?"

"Yep! He really did," I said. "Look at God."

So that was it, the date was final. In approximately fifty days or less, I would become Mrs. Sandra E. Weekes, the pastor's wife (Mrs. SEW). After finalizing the plans, I watched him in joy call all his friends all over the world to tell them his good news. He was getting married to the love of his life. With every phone call, my heart felt good. I could see happiness all over his face. To hear it in his voice just made me smile.

The next day, he went out and bought an engagement ring. I was hoping he would buy my ring before I left the island since he made the announcement to the church. I really didn't want to return home this time without one. Although I got my wish, I was a little disappointed. The ring was beautiful, but it wasn't the "rock" I was hoping for. After all, I was going to be the pastor's wife. Surely I'm supposed to have the biggest diamond in the church. He's an apostle for Christ's sake. I just knew I was going to have the kind of "rock" that, when I raised my hand to praise the Lord, would sparkle in the lights. Ha, Ha, Ha. Wow! Yeah, that's what I was thinking.

The Lord rebuked me instantly. He said to me in a stern voice, "You have never been materialistic; don't start now."

"But, Lord," I sighed.

The Lord said, "But nothing! Don't start now."

I repented before the Lord and asked Him to help me remain humble in this.

"Just stay in My presence," I heard Him speak to my spirit.

"That no flesh should glory in his presence." (1 Corinthians 1:29)

CHAPTER 2
The Middle -
Lies, Trials and Deception

Before I knew it, April nineteenth was here. I had officially become the pastor's wife. I could not believe how quickly my life was changing before my very eyes. Three months prior, I was ordained as a minister. And now, God was doing another new thing.

"Behold I will do a new thing; now it shall spring forth; shall ye not know it? I will even make a way in the wilderness, and rivers in the desert." (Isaiah 43:19)

I was excited about what God was doing in my life. I felt I could scream it from the highest mountaintop. I wanted to share it with the world because God was about to do amazing things in my life. My expectation in God was on a level I hadn't experienced before. I just knew from that day on, everything was going to be perfect because I married the man God Himself chose and prepared me for. I accepted what God was doing with much gratitude. I knew this was God's doing. I didn't fear or worry about anything. After all, I was now the pastor's wife.

Time was spent in Pensacola. My husband and I packed our bags and returned home to the Virgin Islands. Our life here took off quickly after the celebration of our marriage. We had a private reception at the best seafood restaurant on the entire island, Cravin Crab. It is a family owned and operated business. The owner and his family were absolutely amazing. The food was fantastic, and the level of service we received from the Acuna family was absolutely magnificent. The love they showed us was genuine. It was only the beginning of many more things to come.

After a couple of days of rest, my life as a pastor's wife began. We were up very early every morning, going to the church. My husband didn't waste any time putting my hands to work in the ministry, organizing his office, filing paperwork, creating letters, etc. Although this took several weeks to complete, I got the job done, sometimes with his help, but most often without. We started out working together, and then suddenly I was being dropped off at the church alone to complete my tasks. It wasn't long before I felt more like an employee instead of a wife.

I said to my husband one day, "Since I'm here every day, I would really like to have my own office."

There was one that was only being used for storage that would have been perfect for me.

He replied, "I thought we could share my office so I can look across the room and peep under your skirt."

"Excuse me!" I laughed. "My skirt will never be that short."

Laughing, he said, "I meant so I can see your beautiful face."

"Yeah, right. I believe you meant what you said at first."

"Well, you are my wife," he proclaimed.

"Yes, baby, I am," I agreed. Although it sounded sweet,

it wasn't what I wanted. He liked to work in silence, and I am the opposite. I work with music. However, I learned to share his office and play my music at a level that would not disturb him when he was present. As time progressed, we were getting things in order as he desired. It was one project after another.

Then, the meetings started. He had meetings here, there, and everywhere. Being that I assumed most of the meetings pertained to church business, I didn't fret about not being present. I assumed he was meeting with other pastors or people who were conducting business with the church. However, in the months to come, I found out it was the furthest thing from the truth. I discovered that, although some meetings were church based, there were many that were not. I discovered the word "meeting" was just his choice of word to use to seem busy so that I wouldn't question.

When the Lord began to speak to me concerning his "meetings," I found out another definition of the word meeting: to become personally acquainted. To my surprise, he was becoming personally acquainted with many that had nothing to do with church business. So this was where our marital bliss suddenly turned into lies, deception, trials, and tests. I thought, "Oh no, God, three months in and this. But he's a pastor. I'm a pastor's wife; this can't be happening to me." I told God, "But you chose him. What is going on?"

Before I could give the Lord a chance to answer, I decided I was going on a fast. So I asked my husband to join me on a fast. He refused. Not only did he refuse, but he forbid me to fast also. My comprehension to this foolishness was zero. I began to question my husband concerning a lot of things that God was revealing to me in prayer. Although he wouldn't allow me to fast, he definitely could not stop me from praying, at least that's what I thought. The more I prayed, the more

God revealed. I began to ask God to show me the hidden things in my marriage.

Honestly, there were many days I regreted praying that prayer. The Lord showed me my husband lying, cheating, drinking, and using and misleading people. I was angry with him. But mostly, I was angry with the Lord. I could not believe I'd been married three months and my marriage was already in a trial. I really didn't understand what was happening, but I knew I needed to keep praying. I would get out of bed at two o'clock in the morning to seek God's face concerning my marriage.

Then it began. My husband would get upset. He would come upstairs to my prayer room and interrupt my praying, saying, "This is not a good time," or touching me, telling me to get up and come back to bed. Oftentimes, he made the comment to me that God was not pleased that I was leaving my bed to go pray.

I said, "Really? Then why does He keep waking me at this hour if He doesn't want me to pray? I'm an intercessor and prayer warrior, so yes, I do believe God is pleased."

What he said next blew my mind. "Then if you think God is pleased because you're upstairs speaking in tongues and your husband is in bed upset, then you have no idea who God is. You need to control your spirit!" he yelled.

I was flabbergasted, actually, speechless, probably for the first time in my life. He continued to tell me that I had better learn to pray while lying in bed instead of jumping up and running upstairs every time my eyes opened in the night. I was in shock. I began to ask the Lord why he didn't want me to pray. "I don't understand, Lord. I would think he would be happy knowing he has a praying wife. Why on earth would he be upset?"

The Spirit of the Lord spoke these words to me: "Because

he is not spending time with Me in prayer and in My Word. Every time he hears you praying, he gets convicted. He has allowed the sin in his life to blind him from truth. But, Daughter, you keep on praying."

The sad thing was the more I prayed, the worse things got. He began drinking on a regular basis, sneaking around, seeing women in the church and out of church, claiming he had meetings but never allowed me to be a part of them. Adjusting to the island life was hard enough by itself. To add the lies and deception of a new husband, I thought many times that it was more than I could bear.

I was asking my husband why he was drinking. He went from having a glass of wine at home occasionally to wine almost every night. He didn't like being questioned about it. He would encourage me to have a drink with him. I refused on many occasions.

That would make him angry, and he said, "Oh, you think you're so holy you can't have a glass of wine with your husband? I can't believe you don't know how to enjoy life."

We argued about it all the time. One day, I had a drink of wine with him to keep peace in my home. He was excited because I had finally learned to submit to something he was asking me to do. At least that is what he said.

He was happy and the Lord was not. That night, the Lord woke me up at 2:20 a.m., demanding me to get to my prayer room upstairs. Lying in the bed, I said, "Lord, if I get up, he's going to be mad all over again."

"Who would you rather have mad, him or Me?" said the Lord. "Get upstairs, now!"

I jumped out of the bed, not worrying about what my husband would say. He'd had so many glasses of wine, he was passed out. He never knew I left the bad. When I entered into the room, I could feel the Presence of the Lord. The Spirit of the Lord rebuked me in such a way I had never experienced before. I got a good Holy Ghost beating in that room.

When I was able to pull myself together from the crying, sobbing, and snorting, the Lord said to me, "Make it your last drink."

I said, "Lord, he's the pastor and he gets away with having a drink? I'm just the pastor's wife and I get rebuked? Isn't this backward, Lord?"

"I called you to submit, not to be stupid," said the Lord.

"I know, God, but I was trying to have peace."

"Keep your mind stayed on Me," said the Lord. "I will keep you in perfect peace."

"But God, I still don't get it; it doesn't make sense to me at all," I proclaimed to the Lord.

What the Lord said next made me cry all over again.

"My Daughter," the Lord stated, "you can't do what he does. The anointing on your life can not be played with. You can't join him in something I sent you here to save him from. You think because he's the pastor and the apostle, he's more anointed than you. He's not! The sin in his life is taking over, and the anointing is diminishing. He can see the anointing on you, and envy of that makes him discredit who you are in me. He has been blinded by the enemy, and the enemy is after your anointing. But, he's going to push you into your destiny. "

I cried, "Why, Lord? I'm his wife. We're supposed to be a team, not jealous of each other. We're supposed to help each other, complement each other. I don't want him to be jealous, God. I've gone through a lot of fasting, praying, giving, losing, sacrificing, and being used for this anointing. Please, God, help me!"

"Take comfort, my Daughter, in knowing it won't be like this always."

"But I'm the pastor's wife!" I yelled at the Lord. "I'm the last person he should be envious over. This can't be real, God."

The Lord said to me, "It's very real and not just in your marriage, but in many marriages of pastors and wives. That's why I give husbands a specific command concerning their wives."

"Husbands, love your wives, and be not bitter against them." (Colossians 3:19)

"Unfortunately, Daughter, a lot of pastors forget this scripture while quoting so many others."

All I could say was, "Lord, give me strength."

I got off the chair and went back to bed. Just as I lay down, my husband rolled over to pull me close to him. I felt so disgusted. I didn't want him to touch me. But I knew inside I couldn't start acting up. I lay there in his arms thinking, "Oh, my God, I am literally sleeping with the enemy."

The next morning, while cooking breakfast, I decided to test what the Lord had told me the night before. I said to him, "Baby, let me tell you about this amazing experience I had with the Lord before."

"Not right now. Can you just finish cooking so we can eat? It's going to be a busy day, and if you're hanging with me, we've got to get started early."

"Okay, then maybe later," I told him.

"Maybe."

As I sat at the table to have breakfast like we always do, I said, "Why don't you tell me about an experience you had?"

He immediately began sharing a story. I was shocked. As I sat and listened, I thought, "Wow, you don't even want me to talk about how the Lord speaks to or uses me?" I said to myself. "God, how do I live like this?" My marriage was going downhill fast. If I couldn't share a previous experience,

I knew I definitely could not talk about what had happened last night.

Unfortunately, the drinking became more and more often. The more he drank, the more he lied. Every time I saw him making himself a drink, I would start singing praise and worship songs. I could sense his anger and frustration as he sat outside on the balcony. As if drinking wasn't enough to deal with, I also had to deal with the lies and infidelity. Lies on top of lies, woman after woman.

He was continuously texting women all throughout the day and half of the night, using the excuse, "It's ministry. You just don't understand."

He was right. I didn't understand why single women in the church were texting my husband at ten-thirty and eleven o'clock at night when he had a wife they could talk to and a women's president they could talk to. But what I did understand was that it wasn't ministry. He never talked on the phone to them in my presence, only texting. I felt disrespected. He used the ministry to cheat and lied to cover up his cheating.

Whenever I questioned him about the late night texting, he would say, "They're struggling. I'm their pastor. I just can't shut them out."

In return, I would state, "I'm not asking you to cut them off. However, I am their pastor's wife; can't they talk to me?"

"You're not ready yet," he would state.

"I was ready the day the Lord sent me here or He would not have sent me."

This made him angry, and he would yell at me. "Oh, so you want to be the pastor, is that what this is about? You want to take over my church?"

Standing in amazement, I was left speechless. I couldn't figure out where in the hell that was coming from. At this point,

I knew trying to reason with him was out of the question. So, I went into prayer, asking the Lord to show me the truth, to show me the things he was hiding behind the ministry. One night, after returning from a "meeting," he found me already in bed as it was after ten o'clock.

"Good evening," he stated as he entered into the bedroom.

"Good night. How was your meeting?"

"Great."

Mumbling under my breath, I said, "I bet it was."

He went on to say how tired he was, but I noticed he wasn't too tired to be texting someone as he was getting ready for bed. Once he lay down, I rolled over to him, and the smell of alcohol was coming from his pores. I said to myself, "Lord, he's drunk. How on earth did he make it home? Thank You, Lord, for Your grace." I started to position myself back to my side of the bed.

The Lord said, "Be still."

"What?" I asked.

Again the Lord said, "Be still."

I didn't understand why, but I obeyed. A few seconds later, his phone beeped with a text message. Without hesitation, he picked up the phone to read the message. As he was reading, so was I. Since he was intoxicated, he didn't realize what he was doing. But I realized it was God revealing just as I had asked him to do.

It was a young lady in the church texting him, and the conversation had nothing to do with ministry. He responded, asking her if she wanted to swim at Mahogany Run, which was the condo where we lived. Before she responded, he placed the phone on the nightstand and fell asleep, actually passed out.

My heart broke, my whole body felt numb, and all I could do was cry. For the days to come, that's all I did. He didn't know why I was crying all the time. It became so overwhelming for me that oftentimes I would take a shower just to cry.

He had started complaining that I cried too much. When I would cry, he would get angry and beging yelling and shouting, as if that was going to help. Not knowing what I knew, he carried on as if life was okay. After a few restless nights and continuous crying, I brought up the text messages. He lied, of course, but that didn't shock me. However, what did shock me was him accusing me of going through his phone while he was sleeping.

"You have got to be kidding," I thought. "I don't even know the code to your phone." At that very moment, I realized my husband, who is a pastor, had a serious drinking problem. He still didn't know how I saw the message. He went on for weeks reminding me how he couldn't trust me now because I don't let him have privacy. I knew he was just trying to cover up his cheating and lying. But in the midst of all of this, he still continued to drink.

Early one afternoon, while he was cooking lunch and drinking, something happened, and I was totally outdone. He called me into the vanity area of the bathroom. While washing his hands, he said, "If you think I'm lying and cheating, check my phone."

"I don't want to check your phone. That's nonsense."

"Check it! Check it!"

"Baby, if I have to go around checking your phone, then we have a serious problem. I don't want to live like that," I replied.

"Well, you're checking it anyway when I'm asleep," he continued. "You might as well check it while I'm awake. You're accusing me of another woman and you don't even know the whole story."

"Tell me the story, the whole story!" I yelled. "I'm not stupid. I know what I know."

So he began to tell me how the young lady asked him if she could bring her children to the pool to swim. His reply to her was he needed to talk to his wife.

I cut him off saying, "If you're going to continue to lie, we don't have to have this conversation," and I walked away.

He followed me into the living room, picked up his phone, and tossed it to me saying, "Read it for yourself" (not knowing I had already read it). Then it happened; he gave me the four-digit code to unlock the phone.

I was amazed and said to myself, "Yep, he's definitely drunk." I calmly said, "Baby, that is not necessary," as I handed him back his phone. "I don't want, or need, your code to your phone. If you say you didn't invite her, so be it. I don't believe you, but so be it." I then turned and walked away quickly to write down the four number code before I forgot it in all the drama that was happening. As I put the number into my wallet, I began to thank God for revealing truth to me still.

The next morning, he left the house in a hurry, again late for another meeting he supposedly had at seven thirty. In his rushing to get out the door, he left his phone on the counter charging. When I got out of bed and went into the kitchen, I was surprised to see the phone sitting there. While I was contemplating on whether I should or not, I began to cry. I could hear my grandmother saying, "Don't be searching for something that you may not be able to handle when you find it."

In my heart, I knew it was going to be bad. I said, "Lord, what should I do?"

The Lord replied, "My child, you having been praying for the truth to be revealed. You didn't know I was going to do it, but I have answered your prayer."

The enemy came in and said, "So you're so holy and you're going to sneak into your husband's phone behind his back?"

Before I could entertain that thought from the enemy, the Lord said to me in a loud, clear tone, "You are not sneaking, remember, he gave you permission. He gave you the code and said read it for yourself. Now, Daughter, you do exactly that. I am with you. I will comfort you."

I did just what the Lord commanded me to do. I picked up the phone and began reading, only to find out it was more than just that one message, and more than just that young lady. On my, how my heart hurt so badly. For an hour and fifteen minutes, I read messages that my husband was exchanging with over six different women. Lunch meetings, breakfast meetings, and dinner dates that he hid behind the ministry. Not only were there secret "meetings" and text messages, but some had pictures to follow.

He had invited a couple of women to Ft. Lauderdale, as this was where he was going to purchase my new truck. I cried and cried and cried. I discovered all kinds of apps on his phone he used to talk to people all over the place, even a young woman who lived in Pensacola. I could not believe my eyes. I discovered on Tuesday nights, when we had prayer at the church, he didn't go because he was using that time I was in prayer to talk to his many different women. So, while I was at church fulfilling my duties as the pastor's wife, the pastor was home drinking and entertaining women by phone.

After seeing all my stomach could handle, I rested the phone on the counter where he had left it. Crying, I walked to my bedroom to sit down. I took a shower to calm myself down. When I got out of the shower, I began to pack my clothes. I'd had enough of the lies, deception, and the cheating. I started to feel sorry for myself, and I began to pray. While praying for my husband to be delivered, I prayed for the women as well. I thought, "How lonely and desperate they must be to settle for a conversation by phone with a man they would never have. Where is their self-esteem? They know he's married. They would never be able to live in the Virgin Islands; they would never live in my beautiful house, drive my new truck, or lay with him at night. They would never really have his heart, only his spirit of lust, which means what they think is real talk is really just a demonic spirit they're dealing with. How very sad for those desperate dames." I prayed God would boost their self-esteem and have mercy on them.

The Lord said to me, "No need to worry, my child. Vengeance is mine! And they shall reap what they have sown, for they were very aware of his marital status."

I said, "Let your perfect will be done, Lord."

I continued to pack my bags. After I was done packing, the Lord said to me, "Where are you going?"

"Home."

"You are home, my child," the Lord replied. "I know you are hurt, disappointed, and disgusted, but my child, you can't leave now."

"Why? You didn't bring me here for this, Lord. I can't deal with this anymore."

The Lord replied to me, "My child, you are stronger than you think. I have already strengthened you to endure this. I chose you because I knew you wouldn't give up the fight by throwing in the towel and leaving. My child, don't fret. I am with you, and I have anointed you for this. When you feel discouraged, remember my Word."

"And we know that all things work together for good to them that love God, to them who are the called according to his purpose." (Romans 8:28)

I was hurting so much, and I did not want to hear this at the time. However, I knew I couldn't leave.

When my husband returned home, he saw my packed suitcases in the bedroom. "Going somewhere?"

"Yes."

"Where, if I may ask?"

"Home."

"I thought you were home?""

"Well, so did I, but it doesn't feel much like home right now. You know, if you were going to treat me like this, you should have left me in Florida. I was doing just fine on my own."

"So you're leaving me?"

"Yes, I am."

Then, just when I thought I had heard it all from him, he said to me, "Did you pray about that? What did the Lord say?"

Laughing, I said to him, "Are you serious?" However, he was very serious. I could not believe my ears. I thought to myself, "He's gotta be kidding." But then I realized, in spite of his foolishness, he knew that in everything I do, I try my best to be obedient unto the Lord. I chuckled to myself and said, "Lord, there is still hope for him."

He said, "What is it going to look like for the pastor to show up at church without his wife?" "Well, you should have thought about that before now," I replied.

Reaching for my hand, he said, "Darling, let's sit down and talk." Leading me to the sofa, he said to me, "Darling, you know I love you. I have loved you a very long time. Now that I have you, you really think I would mess that up? There is no woman in St. Thomas or anywhere else I want more than you. I didn't desire you twenty years to lose you. You understand?"

"Yes, I understand that, but I don't understand your behavior. I don't understand how you love me so much and hurt me every chance you get."

"Look," he said, "if you think there is another woman, please, let me show you you're wrong. Let me show you how much I love you and want only you."

"Okay. Then you show me."

He led me to the bedroom and said, "Can we start by unpacking your bags?"

"Sure." He didn't know the Lord had already told me I couldn't leave. I only left them packed just to scare him anyway. But I most certainly let him do most of the unpacking.

CHAPTER 3
The Ending –
Deliverance Begins

O ver the next few months, although the drinking hadn't stopped, it seemed that the lying and cheating had. But I wasn't banking on it too soon. I knew he had concerns about me leaving him, so I wasn't fully convinced. The text messaging and phone calls had cut back a lot. All the so-called meetings he used to attend were minimal. He actually started taking me with him to his real meetings. However, I was still on alert. He really was trying to show me I was wrong or he could change. He still didn't know I had been through his phone in detail.

Often, when his phone would ring, he would show me who was calling. He wasn't sitting around the house texting like before, not caring if I was around. Now, when we were home spending time together, we would turn his phone off so no one could disturb our private time. He really was putting all his interest into us and our marriage. I was enjoying every second with him. While I was enjoying my husband, my marriage, and my new life, finally, I still didn't let my guard down. It all felt so right. I thought to myself, "this is how my life should be," especially since I was a pastor's wife.

Within the weeks to come, we did almost everything together. Then, we decided the time had come for me to go to work. I started working at a local bakery shop Monday through Friday from 7 a.m. to 3 p.m. I enjoyed my job. I was meeting new people and learning the language of the island. But after just a few short months of going to work, my husband was back to his tricks. I knew it was too good to be true.

He started picking me up late from work and having meetings again on nights when we had church. When we were home watching TV together, he was back to texting his women. I found out some were the same women from before, while he had added a few new ones to the list. He still had not remembered he had given me the code to his phone. But this time, he was smart enough to erase the text messages. However, he was not smart enough to erase the other apps that he didn't know I knew about. Our time spent together was becoming less and less every day. When we were together, he stayed texting on his phone a lot. This caused us to argue all the time. All of a sudden, nothing I did was good enough. Nothing I said made sense anymore. He complained that I didn't understand him. I didn't know how to dialogue with him anymore. My passion to do anything for him, to please him and make him happy, was out the window fast.

I had to go to work many days, hurt and wondering who he would be with today. I felt as if I was going to have a nervous breakdown. Many days at work, I had to step outside in the back and just cry. My emotions at work changed. What I thought I was hiding, people were able to see through my actions. Oftentimes, people would question whether I was okay. Holding back the tears, I would lie and say, "I'm fine, just not feeling too well."

Many gave me recommendations of different bush teas to drink. If bush tea could fix my problem, I would walk around with a five-gallon pail of it. The stress of him lying and cheating began to take a toll on me mentally and physically. I began to lose weight extremely fast. I was never big to begin with. Then, insecurity began to set in. I was on an emotional roller coaster waiting for a fall. But in the midst of it all, I kept hearing the voice of the Lord say to me, "I will keep thee in perfect peace whose mind is stayed on me."

I said, "Lord, how do I keep my mind on You in all of this garbage? My mind is on everything right now. I need You like never before, Lord."

The Lord reassured me He was with me and it would not be long before He showed up to deliver heal, set fee and restore.

"The Lord will perfect that which concerneth me: thy mercy, O Lord, endureth for ever: forsake not the works of thine own hands." (Psalm 138:8)

I had to really wait on the Lord to deliver me from this. Nothing I said or did to my husband seemed to make him want to do anything different. Problems were getting worse. The drinking was increased even more. He noticed I was beginning to shut down. I stopped asking questions and making comments. I had decided to put it in the hands of the Lord. I was trying to focus on me. I needed to take care of me.

I began to exercise again and eat, even if I wasn't hungry. I started taking weight gain pills to get my average size back. I had lost so much weight I was a size three. I wasn't happy with myself for allowing this to affect me so much. Whenever he left me home alone, I used that opportunity to get into the presence of the Lord.

I praised the Lord like never before. Instead of getting

into the shower to cry, I was now getting in to worship the Lord in the water. I felt God strengthening me each and every time. I could sense God was cheering me on, "Yes, Daughter, that's it. I got your back." The Lord strengthened me in such a way that when he had a drink, I would go outside on the balcony and sing "This Battle is not mine, Lord, it belongs to You." He's the man You called to pastor and lead Your sheep. I'm just the pastor's wife. When he would lie and text women, I would go to my bedroom and play Candy Crush on my phone. I would turn my gospel music on and let him do what he did.

The Lord had given me so much peace, he started to accuse me of having an affair. I guess he realized if he could do it, I could, too. So, there it was. The guilty now trying to turn the tables. When he saw me declining to go with him when he asked, he became suspicious of me. Little did he know, I was declining so I could stay home and pray and worship God. Now, when he left home, he was calling to see what I was doing. Many times, I would not answer even if I was done praying just to make him worry.

I started going to the pool alone, even though I didn't know how to swim. I would go to lunch by myself instead of waiting on him like I used to. This really had him worried. He would show up at my job throughout the day claiming he was in the area. However, I knew what was going on. All of sudden, now he was checking my call log, reading my text messages and going through my chat room that I have with my daughters. It was sad. He couldn't see I was sitting in the peace that surpasses all understanding.

Then, one Saturday morning, he woke me very early saying, "Get up, let's go to the fish market. I want fish for lunch."

"You go ahead, Baby. I don't want to go."

"Why not? You have other plans?"

"Yes, to go back to sleep."

"No, Darling, get up. I want you to go."

"Baby, it's six-thirty. No, I don't want to go."

"You always say I don't have time for you. Well, now I'm trying to spend time with you and you're telling me no."

I sat up in the bed. "When is the last time you heard me say that?"

He had no response.

"Exactly," I said. "You do what you do."

He kept insisting I go. When I realized he wasn't going to let me go back to sleep,

I said, "Okay, I'm going." I proceeded to get out of bed to get dressed. We met in the vanity area. While he was brushing his teeth, I was combing my hair.

He looked at me in the mirror and said, "You know I love you, Darling?"

"You do?" I replied.

"Wow," he said, "usually you say, 'Yes, I know. I love you, too, Baby'."

"Oh."

"That's it?"

"Well, Baby, nowadays I'm not too sure."

Sounding surprised, he said, "Really?"

"Yes, Baby, really."

"Well, I guess I have to fix that," he said loudly.

I thought, "Yeah, right. For how long, another couple of weeks?" I told him, "I will be ready in ten minutes."

Off to the fish market we went. The fishermen go out and catch fresh fish daily. However, if you don't get there early, you miss out. Everyone is at the market before eight o'clock. We managed to get there before the crowd. He bought our fish and took it to the back to have it cleaned. While the workers were cleaning our fish, we sat by the water and talked. There was a huge fish pond in the back, and he was teaching me the differences in the fish. I was actually happy I came. But then it began to rain. I sat in the truck while he decided to stand under the awning. Then it happened, his phone began to vibrate. So, of course, I looked at it, and just as I suspected, it was a woman. I instantly got pissed off. I was thinking if he had left me home, I wouldn't have been bothered with this garbage today.

They were finally done cleaning our fish. He came back to the truck smiling and happy, but noticed I wasn't happy anymore. "Everything okay?" he asked.

"Yes, Baby, everything's fine." I watched him closely to see his face when he picked up his phone as he had noticed the light was blinking.

He read the message and put the phone down. He didn't respond. After driving about five minutes, when he got to the red light, he picked up the phone to respond to the text. Before we made it home, somehow, he created an argument.

I was upset by the text from the beginning, so I was quiet on the drive home. Now that he started engaging in conversation with this woman once again, he started with me being quiet and dialoguing with him.

I told him, "I really wish you had left me at home. I would've been much happier."

"What does that mean?"

"Exactly what the hell I said!"

He was shocked.

"Just get me home, then you can do whatever the hell you want to do. I'm done."

At this point, he didn't know what to do or say because he had never seen me pissed off before, mad, but not pissed. When we reached home, I went upstairs to my prayer room and sat down. He turned on some island music and began to cook. I closed the door and began to pack up some boxes.

After about twenty minutes, he came upstairs asking, "You're not going to help me cook?"

I acted as if I didn't hear him speaking to me. He turned and walked away. Another twenty minutes went by and the music went silent. I heard him calling my name up the stairs. I looked out the prayer room door, and he stood at the bottom of the stairs motioning me to come. I went downstairs to see what lie he was going to tell me this time.

When I stepped into the kitchen, I noticed he had a drink sitting on the counter. "Okay, here we go," I thought. This should be good.

"Why are you upstairs? You always help me cook. What's wrong with you this time?"

"Same thing that was wrong with me the last time," I answered.

"Oh no, you're starting with that again? I can't believe you."

"You must think I'm stupid! You're back to lying and cheating and you don't think I know! You're so busy entertaining women, you don't even realize every time, and I mean every time, you talk or text one, how your attitude changes with me. You must really think I'm stupid!"

Laughing, he said, "No, I don't think you're stupid, Darling. Insecure, but not stupid."

My blood pressure went through the roof. "Insecure? Insecure? Well, if I'm insecure, you made me this way, damn it! Because I sure as hell wasn't insecure when you married me. You know what, just leave me the hell alone and finish with your drink so you can keep talking to your girlfriend. Your spirit of alcohol done attached to the spirit of lust, and you're so blind right now you can't even see it. But that's okay because when God gets through with you..." I turned and walked away.

He grabbed my arm and forcefully pulled me to him. When I came face to face with him, he took both hands and shoved me up against the kitchen wall. The back of my head hit the wall so hard that a small designer plate, which was on the wall, fell to the floor. Pinning me against the wall with both hands, he stood in my face, yelling and shouting at the top of his voice. He was holding me so tight I could not move. He was so close to my face that as he was yelling about not seeing another woman, he literally bit my top lip without even knowing it.

But the power of God stood up in me and I was not afraid. I continued to stare him in his eyes as he yelled and shouted. After about a minute and a half, he let my arms go and backed up. I believe it just hit him what he had done.

He said to me, "You don't have to be afraid."

"Oh, I'm not, not at all!" He didn't know the Lord told me two days previous to this happening that I was going to have to stand up to the spirit of alcohol but to be not afraid, for He would be with me. My husband turned to walk away, and I moved from the kitchen to the living room as he continued with his charade.

He kept saying, "I don't know why you don't trust me. I don't know why you think I'm lying." "Probably because you are," I stated.

"You know how crazy it is for you to think a pastor could cheat on his wife?"

"Just as crazy as a pastor actually cheating on his wife. Which is more crazy, the thought or the action?" I asked him.

Before I knew it, he started throwing plates on the floor in a rage, one after another. I could not believe it. I went to walk away again and he started shouting, "Don't walk away from when I'm talking to you!"

"You need to calm down."

"Don't tell me what to do!" he continued shouting. Then all of a sudden, he just shut up. The room grew quiet. I walked into the kitchen, and he was leaning on the counter rubbing his chest. Rushing over to him, I asked, "Are you okay? Baby, what's wrong?"

He replied, "I'm fine. I need to calm myself." He walked outside and sat on the balcony.

I followed him with a bottle of water, making sure my husband was okay. He kept assuring me he was fine, he just needed to relax for a little bit. I left him sitting on the balcony with the water. I went into the bedroom and began to pray. I was asking God to have mercy on him but to show him his ways. After about an hour, he came inside and lay down on the sofa. I sat on the sofa at his feet. I could see pain on his face, maybe even guilt. I began to rub his feet and pray for him. I knew this now was going to be a problem. Later that evening, he wanted to try to make things up to me. However, I was not feeling it at all. It was at that point I began to recognize the spirit of pride. In every effort he attempted to fix the problem, he never said "I'm sorry."

The following Sunday morning at church was a challenge for me. Remembering what had just happened yesterday and knowing he was about to minister to God's people, I was amazed. But in my amazement, I felt the urge to tell someone what had happened. I kept thinking, I'm on this island alone with no other family and only one friend. Somebody needed to know what was going on with me. In the middle of Praise and Worship, I motioned for one of the ministers to meet me in the back.

As he came to the back, I followed him, and my friend in the church followed me. She was training to be my armor bearer. I explained to both of them what had happened at our home the day before. I explained that the only reason I was sharing this information with them was because I was here alone, and if something were to happen to me, they would know where to start looking. I explained to them their pastor had a drinking problem, and when he was drunk, I didn't know what he was capable of doing.

The minister grabbed my hand and began to pray. The three of us returned to the sanctuary. My friend grabbed her things and walked out, never to return to the church again. She explained to me that she could not sit under that kind of leadership. He could not pour into her spirit under the influence of alcohol. I didn't like that she was leaving, but I understood. I wished I could leave, too. However, I was the pastor's wife. I had to stay. Although she left the church, we remained friends. However, we couldn't spend time together as we would like because my husband would forbid me to do so. She was the only friend I had and I needed her desperately, but my husband fought it on every angle.

Over the next few weeks, the tension at home grew more intense. The drinking, the lying, cheating, and now to add fuel to the fire, physical and verbal abuse. My life was shattered. My husband and I walked around the house for days at a time like strangers, only saying good morning, good afternoon, or good night, depending on the hour. I was broken and doubted God showing up on my behalf, although I could still hear His voice saying, "Hold on, Daughter, don't give up. I am able to deliver you." I knew God was able, I just wondered if He was going to deliver.

I asked the Lord often, "How can the pastor's wife live a life of violence and be who You are calling her to be in You? How do I continue to support the pastor, knowing he's living a lie? He's not living the Word he's teaching. How do

I remain his biggest fan, his biggest encourager, when he's tearing me down every time he has a drink? The Lord said to me one day, "You do it in My strength. It is not the man you're dealing with, it's a spirit. I have given you dominion over every demonic spirit. You are equipped for this battle, Daughter. You shall win; do not give up, and endure."

"For we wrestle not against flesh and blood, but against principalities, against powers, against the rulers of the darkness o this world, against spiritual wickedness in high places." (Ephesians 6:12)

As time progressed, we had good days and we had bad days. Things became so bad that the same minister I had shared my secret with about my husband started coming to our home once, sometimes twice a week, to sit and try to counsel us. My husband's actions began to change because now there was someone to hold him accountable for his behavior. However, it didn't last long. He somehow convinced the minister things between us were fine. There was no need for him to keep coming.

And at no point did the minister ever come back to me to make sure that I was in agreement with this decision his pastor had made. I didn't understand what happened. Then the Lord revealed to me it was a spirit of deception attached to the conversation he'd had with the minister. I was flabbergasted.

I said to the Lord, "Are there any more spirits I should know about? There's alcohol, lust, pride, lying, control, rage, and now deception." I was so surprised at what the Lord had revealed to me. I was having a hard time grasping how a man of God, a pastor, an apostle, could be so overtaken by these demonic spirits and not be aware, yet still stand over God's people on Sunday morning without touching his Bible all week and drinking almost every day, and preach the Word of God. This was absolutely mind blowing.

But it was even more interesting how certain people claim to know God, to have discernment, and to be closer to God than anyone, yet they don't have a clue. They walk around professing the Body of Christ is blind. They're so used to seeing fake that they don't discern the real thing when it's in their faces. And I thought, "Yep, you're exactly right. Know that the Word hits you first in the face as you speak it out of your mouth." I said, "Lord, now I truly understand the blind leading the blind."

The marriage was almost becoming too much for me to bear. God knew it, and He saw fit to give me a release for a period of time. I knew it would not be permanent, nor was I looking for it to be. But God knew I needed a break from the harsh reality of my life. The dirty little secrets I had being a pastor's wife. I needed to be refreshed and strengthened even more to endure this trial. I asked the Lord why my marriage was in such a trial so early in my marriage. The Lord replied to me, "When this trial has reached My purpose, I will deliver you from it."

"But, Lord, what is the purpose?"

The Lord answered and said, "To not only bring your husband into his deliverance, but to push you into your destiny. This trial is going to bring greatness into your life. This trial will cause you to minister to women effectually and passionately."

"Lord, if I have to go through this, please give it to someone else. I don't want to minister to the women if I have to go through this." Then I came to myself and said, "Thank you, Lord. You chose me. But, Lord, I expect you to redeem the time for me. These are not the kinds of memories I want to be making with my husband in our first year of marriage. "Lord, what I have gone through this year most people experience over a thirty or forty year marriage."

The Lord ended the conversation, saying, "For the life that is to come to you, trust Me, it will all be worth it, Daughter."

Within the next week, I left the island on a one-way ticket, as the Lord had instructed me to do. My husband was against me leaving on a one-way ticket, but not against me leaving. He didn't believe me when I told him this was what the Lord had spoken to me. He tried to argue about it, but I just ignored him because I knew he wasn't in a place to hear the voice of the Lord clearly. So I did what I clearly heard the Lord say to me.

As I was packing my bags, I could overhear him on the phone saying, "She's leaving the island for a week or so."

I was quite sure he was making his plans with his different women. He didn't have to worry about me questioning him on when or what he would be doing. At that point, I really didn't care. All I knew was I was headed to Atlanta to my oldest daughter's house, and I was going to be able to de-stress and enjoy my kids and grandkids. Or at least that's what I thought.

However, God had another plan. My first week in Atlanta was spent exclusively with the Lord. I had all of the downstairs to myself, and I was shut in with the Lord. Praising, worshiping, studying, and in prayer for a full seven days. God was doing some stuff in me.

By week two, my husband was calling with concerns of when I was coming home.

I told him, "When the Lord gives me a release. Right now, I hear the Lord saying to me, 'Be still.'" Oh, he absolutely wasn't receiving that. That was beyond his comprehension at the time. But he could not persuade me to return because I knew without a shadow of a doubt what God had said.

To, my surprise he called a couple of men of God whom he knew had an influence over my life. Men he knew I respected as leaders to minister to me. However, I told them the same thing I told my husband, "The Lord said for me to 'Be still.'" They too did not understand.

They knew half of a story that my husband had told them, and I was quite certain it was not all true. They were also pastors looking at this situation from a pastor's point of view. "You're a leader," they said. "You should be with your husband," they said. "Don't let the enemy deceive you," they said. "Go home and trust in the Lord," they said. "God is not telling you to be still, and you're not in your rightful place," they said. "I understand you're hurt and confused," they said. But God doesn't deal in the midst of confusion.

Little did they know I was not confused at all about what the Lord was saying to me, and I was trusting the Lord. That's why I was being still in spite of what they said. They ended their conversation the same way. "Okay, Lady Weekes. I'm going to pray for you and Apostle."

I responded, "Thank you." I had to go to the Lord in prayer for them. "Okay, Lord, now I have three men of God, including my husband, telling me I am wrong. Lord, I know what You said. I heard You say, 'Be Still,' so how is it that these three think I'm being stubborn and disobedient? If they are wrong, God, I need You to deal with their hearts concerning this, because I'm trusting in You, Lord, with my everything."

The next day, one of the men of God called me back. "Prophetess, tell me again what you're hearing the Lord say."

"Sir, the Lord told me to 'Be Still.'"

"Prophetess, have you heard the story of the man of God who was killed by the lion?" he asked. I replied, "I'm sure I've heard it preached before, but right now I can't recall."

He told me to read the story for myself in I Kings Chapter 13. Then he said, "If the Lord is telling you to 'Be still,' I know you'll hear God for yourself. Read the story and let God minister to you, and then you obey the voice of the Lord."

When I read I Kings Chapter 13, I knew God was confirming for me what I was hearing from Him, and He dealt with the man of God's heart, just like I asked Him to do. I remained in Atlanta for a period of thirty days, until the Lord gave me a release to return home.

Upon returning home, I noticed change in my husband. He was concerned with me and my well being. He was concerned about how I felt about a lot of things. I was thanking God for what He had done in his life while I was away. My husband decided we needed to take a vacation. We needed to get away from the island and spend time together, just the two of us, to work on our marriage.

I agreed with him whole heartedly.

We went on the honeymoon we never had, one week away from St. Thomas. No phone, no work, no interruptions, just him and me. It was wonderful. We were able to really sit and talk, and enjoy each other the way a husband and wife should. We laughed, we played, we walked and talked. It was my prayer being answered.

I kept thinking, "What would have happened if I had returned home too soon, not listening to the voice of the Lord?" I didn't know how long this was going to last, but I figured I'd better enjoy it while it lasted because even on vacation he was drinking, so I knew it could change at any time.

I found out I was right. After having such a beautiful week in the British Virgin Islands, we returned home to St. Thomas only for the drama to pick up where it left off in a few short days. I literally was beginning to think my husband was bipolar. He would be the best husband one week and turn into a totally different man the next. I said often to the Lord, "I just can't figure this out."

I heard the Lord say one day, "Read James 1:8 – 'A double minded man is unstable in all his ways.'" This brought me much clarity about my husband. I began to pray for his mind every day.

"And be not conformed to this world: but be ye transformed by the renewing of your mind, that ye may prove what is that good, and acceptable, and perfect will of God." (Romans 12:2)

Although I was praying, sometimes it didn't seem God was hearing my cry, but I had faith God was working in ways I could not see. This entire experience was developing a faith in me I never knew before. God was literally making me live out the Scriptures, and not just saying them with my mouth.

"My lips shall utter praise, when thou hast taught me thy statutes." (Psalms 119:71)

The Lord taught me how to walk in His Word and believe it with my heart, mind, and soul. My marriage was pushing me closer to the Lord. I already had a relationship with God. However, now my relationship with God was stronger and unbreakable, no matter what. I talked to the Lord about everything. As I opened up to the Lord, He let me know that everything I was concerned about concerned Him. I am the apple of His eye. He would never leave me, nor forsake me. He let me know that as long as I draw nigh to Him, He would draw nigh to me. I found myself talking to people less and to God more. I found out I truly have a friend in Jesus. I could tell Him anything and everything and He would keep it between Him and me. Despite the dirty little secrets of my marriage that I was so ashamed of, God never looked down on me. Instead, He loved on me more and more. The more I trusted Him and praised and worshiped Him, the more I felt His everlasting love for me.

Over time, things became worse and worse. The abuse escalated to another scale. I was being told how dumb and ignorant I was. How I could not ever get anything right. I couldn't clean right, cook right, couldn't even talk right to hold a decent conversation. The physical abuse seemed to become the norm. With every drink he took, I knew there would be a problem. He tried to control everything I did and everywhere I went. He wanted to control my phone and who I could speak to.

I lost contact with a lot of people back home because of this, even family members. I had to call my mother and children while I was at work. I received many messages and voicemails from family and friends I wasn't able to respond to. Because of this, this relationship that God was trying to heal and fix became more strenuous. I wasn't able to tell anyone what I was going through, so I just let people think it was me acting funny or acting too good to be bothered. They never stopped to think that maybe I was having a hard time adjusting to the island life and needed time and space to adapt. Instead, many just began to judge and think what they wanted to. I had enough problems to deal with. So I let it be.

My husband was completely out of control while trying to control me. Whenever I would not do what he said, he would throw me out of the house. If I wanted to go somewhere he didn't want me to go, he would throw me out of the house. Not just throw me out, but my belongings also.

He would say, "You can't submit, you need to leave." He would throw my clothes out the door and lock me out until I learned to submit. He threw new clothes in the garbage can outside because I wanted to attend a ladies' function. He told me if I went, I'd better not come back.

I knew he was drunk and figured the alcohol would wear off while I was gone. Well, I was wrong. To keep me from going, he began throwing my stuff out the door, and not in bags. Hangers with clothes, shoes, personal items. He was in a rage and didn't care.

As I was gathering my things out the yard and off the bushes, I just began to cry, "Why, Lord, why?" I tried to calm him down, but he was not hearing me. He went into the house and locked the door. I was pleading with him to let me in and he refused. I kept saying, "Baby, please let me in, Baby, please let me in!" but he did not.

He shouted through the door, "I thought you had somewhere to go, so go!"

I sat down on the steps of the condo outside waiting for him to open the door. Finally, around midnight, he came outside to find me sitting behind a tree. Again, he began to yell, "Why are you sitting outside this time of night alone?" He didn't realize he had passed out on the sofa and the door was locked.

I knocked and called his name, but he did not hear me. All I could do was pray that God would wake him up before it started to rain like it usually does in the night. After entering the house, I thought he would have sobered up. But again, wrong. He continued to yell and shout in my face while pulling my hair. I just gave up. I didn't have the energy to do it anymore.

I said, "God, I know you're going to show up for me soon." The night ended with him sleeping on the sofa and me in the bedroom. This nonsense went on continuously day after day, week after week, month after month. Each time, the situation grew worse. I didn't know what to do, where to go, or who to turn to. I felt so lost, so abandoned, so ashamed, so confused, so unhappy, so afraid, so insecure, so miserable, so hurt, so broken, so misunderstood, so weak, so unworthy, so unsure, so desperate, so needy, so unloved, so breathless.

I said, "God, am I going to survive this?"

Acknowledgments

First and foremost, I want to give all glory, honor, and praise to the Name that is above every name, my Lord and Savior, Jesus Christ. Thank You, Lord, for my life and its entirety. If it wasn't for the grace and strength You have shown me, I would not have been able to make it. You anointed me for this. Lord, I love You more than anything. Lord, I thank You for teaching me what it really means to trust in the Lord and lean not unto my own understanding. Lord, I thank You for showing me, when man didn't believe, that if I trusted You in this, I would come out Victorious. Thank You, Jesus.

To the Fab Five (my daughters) Terlisa Weathers, Chiquera Hardaway, Nicole Hardaway, and Tiffany Logan for their continuous support; Chiquita Millender and my son-in-law, Ira, for trusting the God in me as I chose to live His will for my life. Thank you for understanding and supporting me in every way. I love y'all more that you will ever know. We will always be the Fab 5 plus one. Truly, you ladies are my very best friends. I thank God for the young women you all have grown to be. We need a prayer conference call soon. To Pastor Robin and First Lady Roxanne Smith for imparting in me words of wisdom when I needed it the most; for encouraging me through it all, to listen and obey the voice of the Lord above all. Thank you for your continuous prayer for me and my marriage. Thank you for believing me when I told you, although it didn't look as if I was being led by the Lord. To the Full Gospel Church of God family in Colorado Springs, CO. Thank you for all the prayers.

To Elder Cynthia Brown, my confidant, my prayer partner, my encourager, my friend, and so much more. I don't know how I would have made it through without you. You have lived this amazing journey with me since day one. You encouraged me to hold on more than I can express. Thank you for enduring with me, through my pain and tears. I appreciate you not advising me from your flesh or your own understanding, but only speaking what you heard the Lord say, no matter how difficult it may have been. I thank you for not judging my husband as I shared my story, but always standing in agreement with me for his deliverance. Elder Brown, the prayers, text messages, phone calls, and emails helped me so much during the most difficult time of my life. I appreciate you more than I could ever express in words. I love you dearly and can't say thank you enough. You are truly an awesome woman of God.

Thank God that the effectual fervent prayer of a righteous man availeth much.

www.ingramcontent.com/pod-product-compliance
Lightning Source LLC
Chambersburg PA
CBHW072211090426
42740CB00012B/2486